D0681773

Also by Jorie Graham

HYBRIDS OF PLANTS AND OF GHOSTS

EROSION

THE END OF BEAUTY

REGION OF UNLIKENESS

MATERIALISM

THE BEST AMERICAN POETRY 1990, *Editor*

THE DREAM OF THE UNIFIED FIELD: SELECTED POEMS 1974–1994

EARTH TOOK OF EARTH: 100 GREAT POEMS OF THE ENGLISH LANGUAGE, *Editor*

POEMS AND PHOTOGRAPHS *(With Jeanette Montgomery Barron)*

THE ERRANCY

SWARM

SWARM

JORIE GRAHAM

[POEMS]

THE ECCO PRESS
An Imprint of HarperCollins*Publishers*

Grateful acknowledgment is made to the editors of the following journals in which these poems first appeared: American Poetry Review, New Republic, Conjunctions, Harvard Review, Heat, Poetry U.K., London Review of Books, *and* Boston Review. *A few of these poems appeared in earlier versions in* Poems and Photographs: Jorie Graham and Jeanette Montgomery Barron *(Scalo Publishers, 1998).*

SWARM. *Copyright © 2000 by Jorie Graham First published in hardcover in 2000 by The Ecco Press. All rights reserved. Printed in the United States of America. No part of this book may be used or reproduced in any manner whatsoever without written permission except in the case of brief quotations embodied in critical articles and reviews. For information address HarperCollins Publishers Inc , 10 East 53rd Street, New York, NY 10022.*

HarperCollins books may be purchased for educational, business, or sales promotional use. For information please write: Special Markets Department, HarperCollins Publishers Inc., 10 East 53rd Street, New York, NY 10022.

Library of Congress Cataloging-in-Publication Data
Graham, Jorie, 1951–
Swarm / Jorie Graham. — 1st ed.
p.   cm
ISBN 0-06-093509-X (Paperback)
ISBN 0-88001-695-7 (Hardcover)
I. Title.
PS3557.R214S98   2000
811954—dc21   99-29305

01   02   03   04   05   RRD   10   9   8   7   6   5   4   3   2

Contents

To say I love you is to say I want you to be

(St. Augustine)

SWARM

from THE REFORMATION JOURNAL

The wisdom I have heretofore trusted was cowardice, the leaper.

*

I am not lying. There is no lying in me,

*

I surrender myself like the sinking ship,

*

a burning wreck from which the depths will get theirs when the heights
have gotten theirs.

*

My throat is an open grave. I hide my face.

*

I have reduced all to lower case.

I have crossed out passages.

I have severely trimmed and cleared.

*

Locations are omitted.

Uncertain readings are inserted silently.

Abbreviations silently expanded.

*

A "he" referring to God may be capitalized
or not.

*

(is crying now)   show me

*

is crying now   (what's wrong)

*

in a strange tree   of atoms   of

*

too few   *more*   no wonder

*

Give me the glassy ripeness

*

Give me the glassy ripeness in failure

*

Give me the atom laying its question at the bottom of nature

*

Send word   Clear fields

*

Make formal event   Walk

*

          Turn back

*

Reduce all to lower case   Have reduced all

*

Cross out passages   Have inserted silently

*

is there a name for?

*

glassy ripeness

*

in failure

*

born and raised

*

and you?

*

(go back)   (need more)

*

having lived it   leaves it possible

*

fear   lamentation   shame   ruin   believe me

*

explain   given to

[4]

explain   born of

*

Absence is odious   to God

*

I'm asking

*

Unseen unseen   the treasure unperceived

*

Unless you compare   the treasure may be lost

*

Oh my beloved   I'm asking

*

More atoms, more days, the noise of the sparrows, of the universals

*

Yet colder here now than in

*

the atom still there at the bottom of nature

*

that we be founded on infinite smallness

*

"which occasions incorruption or immortality"

*

(incorruption because already as little as it can be)

*

(escape square, wasted square, safety square, hopeless square)

*

"to all except anguish the mind soon adjusts"

*

have reduced, have trimmed, have cleared, have omitted

*

have   abbreviations   silently   expanded

*

to what   avail

*

explain   asks to be followed
explain   remains to be seen

[5]

TRY ON

*

At the stake
signaling through flames

*

Mastery   scarcity   desiccation   noon

*

Owning
name of
birth

*

The gods that sleep in museums

*

Oh throat chin loan of arms
and loan of eyes
large the debt and the strengthless
weeping

*

Grieve. Have
hope.

*

Have sights truth in them?
Have hearings truth in them?

*

[6]

Covers her mouth to laugh.

Tries to shake ashes off hand.

Mannequin bent at the knees.

*

(constitution   ceremony)

(take that look off   your face)

*

The light's edge moving over the stiff grasses.
The not-waiting of their being in shadow.
The approach of the sunline which is not
an approach. The smell of it—a drying-out of
all nearby air. The secret law
of that.

*

Wings thickly lifting off the hidden
nest.

The sound of a hand-sized stone hitting dry ground
from a certain height.

*

Holding the mind in   like a wish   so deep
for a long   naked   time   triumphant feeling

UNDERNEATH (9)

SPRING

Up, up you go, you must be introduced.

You must learn   belonging to (no one)

Drenched in the white veil (day)

The circle of minutes pushed gleaming onto your finger.

Gaps pocking the brightness where you try to see in.

Missing: corners, fields,
completeness: holes growing in it where the eye looks hardest.

Below, his chest, a sacred weightless place
and the small weight of your open hand   on it.

And these legs, look, still yours, after all you've done with them.

Explain   the six missing seeds.
Explain   muzzled.

Explain   tongue breaks   thin fire   in eyes.

Learn what the great garden—(up, up you go)—exteriority, exhales·

the green *never-the-less*   the green *who-did-you-say-you-are*

and how it seems to stare all the time, that green,

until night blinds it   temporarily.

What is it searching for all the leaves turning towards you.

Breath the emptiest of the freedoms.

When will they notice the hole in your head   (they won't).

When will they feel for the hole in your chest   (never).

Up, go. Let being-seen drift over you again, sticky kindness.

Those wet strangely unstill eyes filling their heads—

thinking or sight?—

all waiting for the true story—

your heart, beating its little song: *explain* . . .

Explain   requited
Explain   indeed the blood of your lives I will require

explain the strange weight of *meanwhile*

and *there exists another death in regard to which*
we are not   immortal

variegated   dappled   spangled   intricately wrought

complicated   abstruse   subtle   devious

scintillating with change and ambiguity

SUMMER

Explain   two are

Explain   not one

(in theory)   (and in practice)

blurry, my love, like a right quotation,

wanting so to sink back down,

you washing me in soil now, my shoulders dust, my rippling dust,

Look   I'll scrub the dirt   listen.

Up here how will I

(not) hold you.

Where is the dirt packed in again   around us   between us

obliterating difference

Must one *leave off*   Explain *edges*

(tongue breaks)   (thin fire)   (in eyes)

And *bless*. And *blame*.

(Moonless night)

(Vase in the kitchen)

FALL

Explain   duty to remain to the end.

Duty not to run away from the good.

The good.

(Beauty is not an issue).

A wise man wants?

A master.

WINTER

Oh my beloved   I speak of   the absolute   jewels.

Dwelling in   place   for example.

In fluted listenings.

In panting waters   human-skinned   to the horizon.

Muzzled   the deep.

Fermenting   the surface.

Wrecks left at the bottom, yes.

Space   birdless.

Light in it a woman on her knees—her having kneeled everywhere already.

God's laughter   unquenchable.

Back there its river ripped into pieces, length gone, buried in parts, in sand.

Believe me   I speak now for the sand.

Here at the front end, the narrator.

At the front end, the *meanwhile*: God's laughter.

Are you still waiting for the true story? (God's laughter)

The difference between what is and could be? (God's laughter)

In this dance the people do not move.

Deferred   defied   obstructed   hungry,

organized around   a radiant absence.

In His dance the people do not move.

2/18/97

Of my life which I am supposed to give back.
Afterwards.
Having taken part in it.
Every now and then looking up at the moon to see how still.
Supposed to take in and then give back.
Oh player of infinite joy.
As if we are inside, for a while.
Along with the gentle lawns of this earth of course.
A sudden rain sweeping the petals along.
And pebbles the rain won't move.
And these bodies someone has put before me.
And this body someone has put me within,
as if its completion,
told to cast spells—oh you know—a look,
the thing preceding you
you then must come upon,
and name—so suddenly.
Underneath, always, the soil that brightens and darkens.
Now refusing you. Later demanding.
But now, now made to live the life entire,
each day snapping shut its eye,
leaning out from the green to whisper—
you too will at last be
free of all trust—
learn the slope, lean into the open spaces, learn the slope,
say no one will take me back,
say I will keep what I have taken from this black earth,
and the sparrows landing, and the small dip of the branch,
and the last village on the highest ridge we came to,

children playing music on their knuckles,
feet skipping, dirt tossed round and then resettling on
                              their prints,
where dance steps are
for just a moment longer
              visible —
the sure-footed already ahead of us on the high mountain pass,
and the great bird in his shelter the sky slowly circling,
and the peaks, up there, shoved up hard
into the weightlessness —
And the instant they are built up into,
and the gone instant, the vector . . .
A god is smiling in his sleep.
Imprisoned inside him the sleep is smiling in a beseeching
                              solitude.
Inside the instant, inside the mind of the invented ones, our minds,
something like a small fragrance, blooming, so fast, straining and straining
                              to stay.
Let the loved glance open up and go, too.
Let it spill out and be taken back.
Let it be disavowed.
But let there be something mute left us that cannot go.
Like a god's mouth held shut.
An intake of breath a delay.
So that the everything, tempted, will push on us,
taking our whole freedom —
weeping too, in its small applause, to take us.
All the rest I swear given back whole.
Never again empowered.
Never again a thing that can come shaped
out of a mouth — the world
put in (have I already let it go) the world
taken back out. So rich now, thoughtless again.
The pillars taken, the roof taken.
The light arch of my belief —

the clay of my space, of my redistribution.
Leave me the thing that will not burn.
Leave me the thing that cannot be thought—I will not
$$\text{think it.}$$

UNDERNEATH (UPLAND)

In haste   about haste

from the   beginning

unguessed back to

all   this   now

(right hand across the fold of the

current garment

folded)

(the light-bearer standing so still   hearing and seeing)

(us still in the Lord's Hall)

(in which we have the privilege of

no rights)

(whether contriving to repair the invisible seam or contriving

to rip it, none,)

cold, slumbering awhile,

world the whole residence (how small),

light-carriers carrying light for the Lord

(who are all these fallen

the light lifted

for us to step over

reveals?)

also the trees it licks and brings up once in a while?

light swinging in the right hand of this me the follower

trying to overhear the low secret though not too hard

light touching everything/grace and slenderness of its touching

as if it would ravage of course   but it won't

made precisely to hold back   (precisely)

while the creatures are felled,

gracing the high slopes with cries and outstretched arms

felled, among the stout-fibered living wood,

felled, the rest pierced through with green,

to make the basilica of divine hazard,

to make the basilica for alien lips among uplands

and indeed further,

all the way to where the prince is mistakenly hunted

by his own,

where the folk of the land

stand for sorrow and gleam with

the thieving of   their Lord

who weeps for them as he thieves

to give them their right freight of woe,

the thieving a spell to release them from unbelief,

to place them smack in hand, vague, chased,

unkenneled creatures howling,

earth-floor   anguish,

small noise of the parallel streams,

someone in a corner weeping,

elsewhere, free of any mind, a bitter dream,

a wounded ankle, boughs brought lower for an instant,
                                        grappled,

no troubled stream of

narrative

just the one good fight within the range of vision of

the savior

And his fury. Mid-morning. His constantly westing

drooping eye, his vestal, distracted

unchoosing.

THE VEIL

Exile   Angle of vision.

So steep   the representation.

Desperate   Polite.

A fourth wall   A sixth act.

Centuries lean up into its weave, shudder, go out.

Tongue caresses its entireties.

Look closely for the adjusting of wings,

the knife removed from breast, the noose from

neck,

the acid slippers of eternity being tried on each new foot,

and the patience of understudies, the curtain that cannot rise or fall

over the depth of field. Oh love.

What war did we hope for?

What sleep?

Couldn't the orchestral die down a while—

burning bushes, moving vans—little plazas—eyes of the lion?

What if the rear-view were to open up?

The whole unseeable back where the blood flows off,

drying so quickly,

us broom in hand trying to sweep the front porch off,

every now and then looking up to see how soon.

How soon?

The clouds haul off across.

We tidy up. (*I see*).

War then tidying-up then war. (*I see*).

Shovel the rubble to the roadside. (*gesturing*)

Let the carts loaded with interpreters
                         get by.

It is years.   Goodnight says

the heaven at our backs. (*points*)

Greatness   is sleepy.

Oh my stringed-thing, throat,

when was it I first took this pencil and wrote out

this emptiness you hold now to your ear—

listen: the other place is in it still.

The drawers are full.

Nothing scares off.

I knock on the front

whispering open up, forgive us,

can you grow any more silent?

The windows glint to me

re the straight paths of the right hand,

the refusal that anything be measured
                        or judged,

up here in the shiny
        democracy,

the so-called cup of bitterness,

the so-called train

picking up speed, the so-called

sublime it flatly aims for—

Are we alone? I can never think of you
                    without smiling.

UNDERNEATH (SIBYLLINE)

As if we could tell

if we'd been abandoned.

The battle took so long that soon between the enemies
                            the bonds
emerged.

Also slowly extinguishing: the sounds of birds, the barking
of dogs.

Planets howl.

Musics rise and fall below the battle sounds.

And you, one being with two parts:

there exists only one instant in which

you can both gain and lose your life.

Remain seated says the voice-over.

(Shouldn't the red light blink?)

Corridor   Curiosity

Appointment   Time

Gods defeated or perhaps   in fact—

(I can smell it, can't you?) —

What would you like, someone asked long ago.

Ancient, I'm ancient the one in line before me screams.

I haven't given up on you darling, the hum replies.

I'm planting a wildfire

in your head,

I'm watching I'm remembering,

even though you're dead, you know, you're old tricks —

And this office is swarming with talent.

But what would you *like*?

To stay in your skin?

You've got all of us turning inside-out for you,

but what is it you're suffering from? —

blinking on and off

in the margin,

the free race,

where I goes without saying,

where it begs the question?

Oh bend.

Open your hiding places.

Burn all the letters.

Look in the ashes with both hands.

Finger in there for any bits intact.

                    Wrist-deep

in the fine grains, so cold,

feel further round for fragments,

for any last unburnt

piece of

the crashing of mind,

or any promises (so parched) come down through the sentences
                                        to breathe,

pushing the few bits back to the tiny fire,
                    the struck match,

and worrying, and keeping each fragment lit to the very end

by turning it

to every side   every last side —

Look you have to lift the match to it again

because this syllable   is still intact.

PRAYER

(after Holderlin)

Should we not speak of you?
Should you ring in us   as an idle caprice

pressed into   service,
should we not, you deed rampaging destiny, furious,

pressing voice into service,
as if the hurling of hot arrows,

pressing the good into your service,
making it play for you?

And yet you will veil our eyes
that we not perish.

Hard burden. Names and names.
Likewise the river.

I called you once and thought you once.
You travel down to me on your allotted paths,

a light embrace, miraculously omnipresent.

THE SPECTATORS

The impatience of the spectators

cannot be relieved.

It rains. Roof leaks.

God stands in the corner.

The crowd overflows

to get a better view.

It rains. Thought leaks.

Now impatience grows its own corner.

Whatever happens comes your way.

Distance leaks.

The last possible instant

wells up, root dangling

that would take root.

Some of the eyes are bandaged with rain.

Some of the eyes wait for the gun to be fired.

Of course there is a starting point—

something which says I too waited, part of the crowd,

unable to discern being ahead

from being behind,

unable to afford the dangerous.

Spring passes into summer.

Has friends. Has acquaintances.

Let us proceed

to the loss of independence.

To the peculiar unfinished look of the place,

the plausibility   of the glory of god,

the small town   where the hero was born,

us shooing young hens off the monument.

Yes she loved him very much.

Yes she knows what the two things are.

Oh drowsiness.

Crackle of pages turning.

The stench is lovely, everywhere.

And continuance itself, implacable.

And the examiner checking the tags.

And the rosebush dead.

And the enemy dead.

Wouldn't you like to see the shrine, a favorite?

We can be received at any hour.

UNDERNEATH (ALWAYS)

Who sits with me?
Once I thought to think till opened-up.
The frost in the distance takes in light.
In front of my eyes day and night appear.
They act like truth. They come at me.
I am weaponless do they not know it.
There is a god here but it is not shaped.
Is moving around us, sometimes shines from afar, is not
a pure thing.
Also in it a purring. Never a beckoning. Only sometimes a purring.
How much difference among things it aims to show.
Once morning sent arrows.
Now it is anecdotal.
Go loveliness.
Diminishment I find thee here and there unclear.
Yet your eyes *are* thinking as I look in
Still living so I push in.
Sidelong, I do not miss
how the yellow beam tonguing across it
cannot even touch the porch.
It is not lost on me.
The arrow *does* arrive,
just not in time.
Not in time, as at tomorrow's trauma-center, say.
Not in time, as the dancemaster scolds.
Do you not hear the time? Do you not listen?
But, master, I've gone a far way down your path,
emptying sounds from my throat like stones from my pockets,
emptying them onto your lips, into your

ear warm from sunlight.
Not in time. My suit denied.
What is lateness my small heart asks.
More later says the light. More. More than you think.
Time now for bread pushed into the mouth,
bending to refill the water-bowl.
When a bird dips through I look into you again to see
your figuring of it, the outwardgoing of your blindness
where the arcing seems to streak your gaze.
But not in time. Sight never happens.
We call the day Saturday.
At dinner I try again,
looking through the end of afternoon into your glance,
two rips you keep repairing.
How much left out?
Who tore   what's left   bitter the I
More bitter yet the sewing back together.
How it must be done by laws in unison.
And not in time. Oh
I'd as lief not leave, my earth.
However far I've gone
all that remains is where I began.
Look, crane a bit love, look:
not even a beginning in it.
Not the trace of a setting-off.
What grows is the feeling of difference.
Even muscles shrink back from it.
Even the skin wants out from light.
Only the sockets hold and hold.
Can you let the self back in again, cold skull?
There is the purr again, only across the vale this time.
And then the train, of course, the 6 o'clock
going again from there to there.
Once upon a time, I think.
We call the day Sunday.

5/3/98

When do I say   yes

And it become again a form of joy?

A sound like water.

A large bucket lifted and poured.

I can still hear water.

No I can still remember.

What isn't true but must be believed?

What isn't   but must be.

How strange.   A mind made up.

Say the words you should have said.

Say what you would have meant.

Say what you   mean.

Disguised as thoughts.

Ruins.   Sentences.

Self-evidence, then story,

then where they take one chair

away.

DESERT/DUNE

Centuries possibly although you can't tell from here.

As if your gaze could finger its linkings one by one—

the grains, the change, the blazing
                        infinitesimals.

So much time has passed.

Can't you feel its adjectival backbone slither,

grainy shifting and reshifting,

as if constantly tired again of being just the world—

describe, describe—

push certain freedoms, bulging, aside,

cast this strictest glance   great bridal veil

over the body of the dune

which moves on under it like the great wave it is,

changing the shine on the ridge of its back,

birds coming down if one is still—

there are not many truths—

till morning comes till evening comes,

till morning comes till evening comes,

wind bursting up like flames off dune—

a wind aflutter on his animal—

riding and riding his one long animal,

sharpening flanks—

the good, the wrong, maybe the free,
                    maybe even some

(softest of all) in-

difference: moon-liquors gentling it—

black fin—fugue of—

and then this side of it, and then that side,

heat seeping from the pressing grains,

some give,

after a while some deeper bend.

I beg   your pardon.

Shrivellings of place now flying from the dune,

spent-living creeping from it—right off the tightened skin—
then tracks unblossoming, then even more spent living
flying off, night airs, insolvent distances, beckonings of wind

to sand, invisible crowd, dust-risen faces—

a metal clang now on the evening air—(oh caravan's
                              unseen

approach):   (syncopation of driest hooves),

(battering of single drum)—(3/5 repeats)—
                    (into dusk air)—

then cooling sand, then crack of voices riding by,

some laughter ticked-out over sand,

deeper and deeper into the open,

following the seriously wounded narrator.

PRAYER

What of   the quicksand.
My desperate eye   looking too hard.

Or of the eye   of the world
looking too   hard

for me. Or, if you prefer, *cause,*

looking to take in
what could be sufficient—

Then the sun goes down   and the sentence

goes out. Recklessly towards the end. Beyond
the ridge. Wearing us as if lost in

thought with no way
out, no eye at all to slip through,

none of the hurry or the between-
hurry thinkings to liquefy,

until it can be laid on a tongue

—oh quickness—like a drop. Swallow.
Rouse says the dark.

MIDDLE DISTANCE

This is certain.

Dream has no friends.

Bottom is there but depth conceals it.

Centuries cannot see us.

Here, in liberty.

(enter others)

What are these eyes for?

What are these hands for?

I have been listening. A long time (looks around)

The "frontier labyrinth" (gestures)

All the people in history (gestures further)

The heart in my throat (spotlight on wilderness)

Then their eyes were opened and they knew and it
vanished from sight.

This is certain.

Dream

will not vector

is illegitimate

hangs over us huge dry wings

suffers with us   grows worse

is not identical with awareness

often lies under the cathedral floor

ought to spare us

oh surely it ought to spare us

entertaining brevity like a sweet curiosity

always the wings opening and closing at a
                    constant rate

as if nothing were happening

never beckoning or imploring why do we
                    stay

has a sharpness, is raven-dark,
    perhaps weak eyesight

is humble   is authentic

(though of course in the inaudible)

usually in bed at night the wings
            tie down

you can hear them like a growing
            of the dark

although all of it of course stays the same

(none of the letters have been saved)

This is certain: inwardgoingness of the
                                        soul

that won't lie down

vague gods

no possible restoration of order

bright city held at the hinge of
                        the wings

remembered touch   weary hands

flame snapping the air in

its one body of bright singularity

dust on the fire becoming fire

and how we shall be obedient

dust on the fire

on the seeming

apple in hand

in the wake of the wings

("speechless sorrowing of Nature")

(you will get lost   you will be left)

bending over looking for the trinket lost

(most quiet heaven)

pale light of the reasons

soul walking in circles

weary scribe

Fly I say, reins in the
        one hand
you now dislodging centuries
        need me
by offering yours suddenly   to free

Wheel without faces on it

Happened   to be

UNDERNEATH (CALYPSO)

1

Sing to me of time and time again

being driven off course

to face another audience

bewitching craving to hold

him   back

I apologize to coincidence

I apologize to necessity

Let happiness try to receive the dead

Apologize to the war I steal him from

You must forgive this veil

It's like a laughing time and again

I wanted to be everything

I know nothing can justify the veil

Be brave Let it descend

Why should the exile   return home?

Era?   Period?

Discover: Calypso has shuffled the deck.

Has veiled the early with the late.

Has veiled sequence.

Remembering violent   as it must be,

and it all now middle-time.   Sleep, love.

What must be   inferred under

the blemished   mantling   shimmers.

How else to keep you.

I apologize to history.

I covered the story with all these words.

Overgrown with eyes.

3

The stress and drag of looking.   Look.

Shuffled the deck   to veil phenomena, yes.

Strike me says each thing.

Resurrect me   in *my*   flesh.

Do not pass through me.

4

Look how our mouths   are bared.

And those, still strapped in their seats, the others.

I am held to myself   by force.

No voyage   home

over blossoming's   broad back.

Forced down instead   into the stalk.

Let your soul slip through   radiance

Let not radiance cling to you   Push through

5

How we walk the aisle: in flames.

Frothing time back   into its corner.

In anguish here   under the veil.

Going broken   before some altar.

DAPHNE

Pick   a card.

Wrong again.

Interrupt   belief.

Write down   hope.

Move lips in sleep.

Widen.

Translate.

Be   less.

Be found.

Be   muzzled.

Say   write hard answers on me.

Bear down   make clear.

The moon rises.

Will never be perfect.

Be good   open mouth.

Don't scream.

Let light come into   taste light.

Earn.

Turn if it's allowed.

Be outstanding.

Give pleasure away.

Give trust away.

With your mouth   loosen everything.

(Music in the distance)

(A man sleeping under a tree near noon)

Let the other mouth seal yours.

Let the other mouth heal yours over.

Run out of air.

Don't break seal.

Break

faith.

Let the given tighten.

Be the experiment.

Forgo explanation.

Touch pain   with great curiosity.

Move from one excuse to the next.

Let your ankles too be tied.

Lapped by that water   injustice

be land   pierced through.

Carry acceptance in you

the aftersound of something felled.

A long time.

Invisible basilica your willingness its floor.

Rope burns   holding the dwelling.

Listen the wind does not slacken.

Pliant bending of the elms.

Wisdom   bruise and fracture.

Lean low to your high office.

Lean back

for the leafing-over.

Install   violence.

Mark   years.

Let not one thing be

outlined by clarity.

This really happened.

This time it was me.

These would be the last motions

of this particular civilization

So listen,

there is a reason,

then there is murder

sleep   forgetfulness

A train passes.

The last one till tomorrow.

Ink makes a sound.

Here   listen.

Play with me   then discard.

Or put it this way:

Do not dream.

Stay awake for the end.

EVE

Noon: something enters
and begins, small, hissing *if, oh if* . . .
I hear it as it stops.

Mid-noon: listening
without the push of listening.

Full sun: walls down,
the wrought-iron gate intact.
I step through. I step back.

Just now: like a feeling
behind one's back.

*

Can't remember:
what this reflection on the water
holds as neither face nor water.

*

Noon: your glance invents for me my glance.

*

Still noon: it is not clear how much
this green, looked-out upon,
tumbling towards the eye   to land   is dressed —

*

Bless, blame, transvaluate—
Change context—
Unexpect   context

*

Step back step through

*

Why do you seek the dead among the living?

*

All day the green,
a sound like silk unspooling from the bolt—

Looks back at us gradually
Increases its speed.

What fell from your lips?

And the mirror, that exit wound—
as living as not?

*

And what fell from your eyes?

As living as not?

Look back? Increase speed?

[4 9]

Explain   *and were you lost*
Explain   *and were you saved*
Explain those who enter as though born

                              *

Yes, he said, because he knew
the deliberate anti-climax
by heart, *yes*,

disorder my clothing,
count my ribs,
hide your face.

TWO DAYS (5/2/97 – 5/3/97)

Full moon; lays his hand
onto her throat, into his mouth
takes her whole ear.

Noon: this pen hovers
over this empty page. One is
free to forget.

Noon. The gate fills to
its edges with the two sides of
opening. Move.

Noon. Regardless of
the gate, buds open all around,
stare at each other

Noon: evaporation is taking
place.

Full moon: your body before me
a nameless hill.

Full moon· seeing, being-seen;
the cold lies in us all night long

In one spot most especially.

I am not seeking altitude.

Noon: we push until
like a third party

matter rages between us.

Noon: pushes us
into the midst to where
Spring stops.

Noon: pushes us
to where a crown emerges and begins to lower
all round our bodies
tiny rips of buds.

Noon: then even the buds push out
into this emptiness.

Noon. The only heaven plays and leaps.

Dusk, with its downslope,
a bride, and one above her
all shivering of mind.

Late dusk: a communication
between what exists and what
is visible (that shore) (who knows

what can be said)—

Full moon;
lays his hand onto her throat, into his mouth
takes her whole ear.

UNDERNEATH (7)

Mirror Roll away
the stone, unrip the veil. Re-
pair.

And handle me.
Behold my hands my feet.
That it is I, myself.

Mirror: a thing not free
it's seeking reply
from.

Mirror These are not questions,
these glances coming back
for more.

The repeated vacancy
of touch
begging for real work.

Door ajar.

Bone so still a guest.

Touching you in sleep
along the lips I start to wake.
Inundation.

Fear being mistaken.

A thing not free we seek

reply from.

Reach your fingers here.

Reach your hand here.

Blessed are those who have not seen
yet have
believed.

Oh look closer. . . . Kneel.
Is it as new as you thought it would be?
As faithless?

Mirror—
Crashsite—
Fear being

mistaken.

See that it is *I*, myself,
repairing the rip it's making as it goes—

the feeling behind your back—

the bough springing back into the tree.

FOR ONE MUST WANT/
TO SHUT THE OTHER'S GAZE

What are you thinking?
Here on the bottom?
What do you squint clear for yourself
up there through the surface?

Explain   door ajar.
Explain   hopeth all.
Explain   surface   future   subject-of.

Pierce.

Be swift.

(Let's wade again)

(Offstage: pointing-at)
(Offstage: stones placing themselves on eyes)

Here: tangle and seaweed

current   diagram   how deep?   I have

forgotten.

Don't leave me. I won't.

Of course.

Explain   saturated.
Explain   and I had no more eyes.

[5 5]

(Oh did they really cross the sea)

Even the least
Even the last

This is certain

(of course)   (take up the arms)   (name the place)

The real plot was invisible.

What are you thinking?

THE SWARM

(Todi, 1996)

I wanted you to listen to the bells,
holding the phone out the one small window
to where I thought
the ringing was—

Vespers scavenging the evening air,
headset fisted against the huge dissolving

where I stare at the tiny holes in the receiver's transatlantic opening
to see evening-light and then churchbells

send their regrets, slithering, in—
in there a white flame charged with duplication—.
I had you try to listen, bending down into the mouthpiece to whisper, hard,

can you hear them (two petals fall and then the   is wholly
changed) (yes) (and then another yes like a vertebrate enchaining)
yes yes yes yes

We were somebody. A boat stills on a harbor and for a while no one
appears,
not on deck, not on shore,
only a few birds glancing round,

then—before a single face appears—something
                      announces itself
like a piece of the whole blueness broken off and thrown down,
a roughness inserted,

yes,
the infinite variety of *having once been*,
of being, of *coming to life*, right there in the thin air, a debris re-

assembling, a blue transparent bit of paper flapping in also-blue air,

boundaries being squeezed out of the blue, out of the inside of the blue,
human eyes
held shut,

and then the whisking-open of the lash—the *be thou, be thou*—

—*a boat stills in a harbor and for a while no one*
appears—a sunny day, a crisp Aegean blue,
easy things—a keel, a sail—

why should you fear?—
me holding my arm out into the crisp December air—
beige cord and then the plastic parenthetical opening wherein I

have you—you without eyes or arms or body now—listen to

the long ocean between us

—the plastic cooling now—this tiny geometric swarm of
openings sending to you

no parts of me you've touched, no places where you've

gone—

Two petals fall—hear it?—moon, are you not coming soon?—two fall

UNDERNEATH (1)

Painful to look up.
No. Painful to look out.

Heard the bird hit the pane hard.
Didn't see it. Heard nothing
drop.

To look out past the shimmering screen to the miles of
grasses.

*

Wind-hurryings.
Low-lying of stoppages.
No Reason.
Always tried knew how to try.

*

Birdcall in the farthest windsounds: atoms.
Opening to it: atoms.
Smaller birdcalls   interruptions
In the swellings   and droppings-off

of current-gush: atoms.
Always.
The sun on the miles of tall-grass seed-tips.
The screen glimmering the world into a silver grid.
Inside the grid nothing complete. Everything that was plunging
                                        now runny with
organization —Fence grass wind gate

open gate or closed.
Distance.
Near noon all the tall grasses for an instant stiff at
attention,

then a sturdy nervousness from left to right—
deep bending of the light—
light carried across on the backs, in on the tips—
the screengrid forced so deep into the eye it's in
disappearance—or the mind—as

you   will
have   it
No   where
No   two

silvers alike although all bendings or bowings
identical
except for the fact of
difference

As in
Yes Sir

where the raven suddenly wetly and rawly
roughens the low vacillations of various windsweeping
hushings—as if he's clawed
a thing truly all the way to

atom and taken it
from here
leaving behind again only bendings
in wind—
and circlings and circlings and circlings and circlings—

the ruling class
of what was
said

grass turned

you tripped up
cried on the phone

someone told
their dream

the full moon
is awaited
this night

what's its name?

and that one does not kill

and that one does not kill

look   it is dead

there is   sun all over it
like a moneying up of it

sparkle

*

You have whispered it all to me but I
wasn't listening you were too
close for me to make
out in-

dividual words all I
heard was the wind rushing into my
opening the ear like a field splaying

all this way then
that as you took in
air to make

the next phrase which
was also atoms—sparkling—meaning—
while the whiteness of
the walls my eyes—
(the only part of me
not yet held down
by you)—my free

eyes, scanning and rescanning, watch,
                    darkens into
corners—your
teeth and lips holding my
whole ear   of joy   also

your hand over my
mouth   in the century   of possibility

yr voice not such   the sun entering
yr saying   the hotel window
so filled with   from the street

yr exhalation   and cries on it
it drowns itself   strangely the right color for
drowns in the *mine* of   cries

itself—all desire   crossing the history
yielding to secrecy   of inwardness vs insideness
spume of syllables   the seepage of

we were hungry   this was our century

hungry for   hungry from
(century)   (century)
            yr hand now

(actually over)   my throat

UNDERNEATH (2)

ghosts   not having
lived   alive now

     it   possible
    eventually

explain   calm

explain   vision

explain   property

also   summer   compromise
as   soon   as

explain   hidden life

explain   echo

also which flower is
heaviest   how it
has   any bearing
on   color

explain   energy

bear   waste

explain   place

explain   accident

    after gods

     is born

      (fall)
     (I'll catch)
      (you)

I'm asking   for weight
The Ready   flowers

UNDERNEATH (3)

explain   given to
explain   born of

explain preoccupied

asks to be followed
remains to be seen

explain preoccupied

mind all summer long filling with
more atoms more day
noise of the sparrows
of the   universals
have you counted the steps

have you counted your steps

is crying now

(is crying now)

(is crying now)

begin again

in a strange tree   of atoms   of

wrong afterwards again show remember freedom

(which will be mine of   the atoms?)

        go back
        need more

having lived it leaves it   possible

explain inseparable   explain common

(the phone rings at dawn) (very occasionally)

UNDERNEATH (8)

1

*

Exhale   (in years)

*

The shadows   live

*

Fleshless   lovers

*

The tabernacle   of

*

(fleshless lovers)

*

(with no lifetimes   laid hard on them)

*

As in they shall seek death

*

and shall not find   it

*

What if there is   no end?

*

What if there is no

*

    punishment.

*

As in   *it is written.*

2

While gods sleep   she says

deposit   in me   my busyness, flesh.

Deposit   thirst   in me.

Deposit   tongue   poor rendez-vous.

And eyes   patient   their dry study.

Also   heavy rains   tearing the soil.

Also   my heart   multiplying terror.

And twelve weeks of summer.

And   an assignment   clear.

Deposit in me.

First shoots.

Unripen what   to ripen my assignment.

Make the sore   not heal   into meaning.

Make the shallow waters   not take seaward   the mind.

Let them wash it back continually onto the shore.

Let them slap it back down onto the edges of this world.

Onto the rocks. Into light unturned by wave. Still sands.

Deposit back on the stillest shore all messages tossed.

Do not take   back in   the soundtrack.

Let the cities stay where they were shouted out.

Let the horizon   lower its heavy   lid.

Agree   to be   seen.

Deposit   silt

Dream of   existence.

Refuse   rescue.

Overhear   love.

3

Where definition   first comes upon us   empire.

THE LOVERS

While the pale moon rises dig a ditch.
Dig a ditch while you still can.

Find the breathing left in winter.
Find the muttering under the kiss.

Remember from the ditch the room, them in the room.
The bright brief hatchlings buzzing the pane.

Remember from the ditch
brief strips of sunshine playing the dirt.

Sing, by the ditch, recall early wonder.
The fingertips eagerly gripping the pen.

Sing, sway, recall
whatever held you tongue-tied, child, and stirring.

Beg mercy   appetite.
Oh brilliant drowning.

UNDERNEATH (LIBATION)

Look   the middle period.

Where will the council be tomorrow.

Where will tomorrow

offer prayers to.

Disperse question-marks.

Know what you write of.

Very tired.   Speak of.

It is morning it is evening.

Murmur names little exiles.

How many syllables   is your nation?

How pronounce it?

Who first spoke it?

Is it the third or the other world?

Could it be mistaken for a book?

Or sadness?

Or a path turned to mud?

Or the hunter who is hunted?

Somewhere in the audience

something not human.

If anything is real then this is real.

The fires burn all the way down

from their mouth   the one war.

Hadn't it seemed eternal,

the one war?

With your mouth now

bear in   mind.

The one who acts must suffer.

Who rules the house?

Persuasion

UNDERNEATH (EURYDICE)

How neatly you describe the thing

tongue in my ear

under the crown one wears when done

playing with ashes which will not rise again

although matter goes on just fine without transformation

the gold-foiled crown or the cardboard if you like

as you see fit   hands of dirt

birdshadow from outside flicking

a bit over the crown if you move around

I like it when the shadows whisp into your ear

I like submission to such untouchable authority

as if my self were a fracture filling up with shadows—

if you think of them, as the sun moves them round,

they are the ashes we were meant to play in,

nothing representable—round earth—lovely game—

or maybe now it's the words read out to me

held up in the sun by your hands of dirt

which look from this distance like hands of fire

gripping their page yet not consuming it

only your voice around us rising higher

as if the words (spoken) were the one thing growing warmer

although the sun on the hands *is* bright

and where it hits the paper even quite blistering—

it makes my head hungry to see the free characters

of the words you haven't read yet waiting from this distance,

there, across the room, crown now in later light

made of the fact of time and submission and event

as we turn the page and meaning follows

as if beauty flowed through us as if we were a gap

in the page, a crack near the center,

without reality, though being spelled out—

Cover me up, be king,

let no one see us here whitening in the century,

two ghosts, their minds filling up with sunlight,

eyes following the motion of the still-golden hands

"but we desired Macedonia" Lord

wanted each of us our very own war

deemed stasis unscalable

light as a sunpatch your hand on my thigh

for one time only not among strangers

trembling the phrase as you read it out

silence by silence the listening filtered

oh for the majesty   of uninterrupted night

earsick   having to use our hands—

follow the clue listener you will go nowhere—

which is close to our heart (take bait) (list

            maiden name) (till it's becoming song)—

whereinall the utterer puts down the paper—

come, find the distinguishing marks

come, make the distinguishing mark

threshing the body I can still lay before you

adrift on disappointment on expectation

who sang   what pulse   clad in fear

which will cure what

as nights ripen   and fall off

into our flesh

and narcotic the waiting

and merciless

for there is in addition   a body

of rites   and customs

how neatly silence describes the thing

UNDERNEATH (WITH CHORUS)

Citizen   Sacrifice

My sacrifice: what shall I use

Face dawn and pour out

What shall I use

What offering sufficient

Say act

Be called

What shall I use

Both hands your voice

Coins gathering in us

Do you not see the hands

reaching and touching: as if to defend the object

Your words are terrible

Have they a king

Could a messenger be sent

How can eyes sense enough

truth under names

What do you mean

I dare not act

Citizens must sanction

What orders   have you

(Being born at last

Do you feel no shame?)

What is the name of the place we have entered

Why do we need the safety of the altar

Surely you know

Blind as you are

What is asked is bitter

Have we not talked enough

Yes we are innocent and deserve help

Where are my words they die away as I speak them

The pain of my eyes is piercing

I feel your presence beside me

I know your voice in the blackness

Why should I see

Oh narrow crossroad

What is it that you beg so urgently

A beginning?

A delay?

To have the god reveal to me my duty

Obedience is hard

No good life endures beyond its season

Do you know why I yield

When I have heard your reason I will know

FUSE

(THE WATCHMAN, *Agamemnon*)

1

It is a sentence   the long watch I keep.
The appearance of me.   Forgive the absurdity.
On this high spot   chains grow strong.
On this high spot   fighting to stay awake.
Knowing by heart   the stars
on lampblack   and how they keep by me all day.
Also the rosebush   scent and apology,
rising red from its own tomb   to my
staring day and night   for a flare not of my own imagining,
to thread its syntax, fire by fire, down
through rocky throat, heart, groin   to here,
to my very foot   here,
to this business of waiting beneath the blurred stars for the
                          one string,
irreversible. Always drowsy. Never spelled.
For a full hour once just stared at one rose.
Up-flaunting, irregular, winged, without any soul.
Mornings it emerging from shadow to tell its one story over.
Sightless facing. I try to learn from it disinterestedness.
How to drive a point home where there is no point. Or home.

2

Strange sweetnesses,
               sketched-in more rapidly at times by skittish winds
                        against your wall,
abstract yet always perfectly
explicit in your rising un-
          repeatable gestures—

unlike the sentence of individual fires I watch for,
that the long coastline be dressed by endings —
by the burning (city) — by the thinking it forces down to me, here, one
                                                  phrase,
one, from burning mouth to breaking heart,
a kind of opulence, yes, but then of course ash . . .
Whole days I love to press my stare
                                        onto the gorgeous agitation
                                        of your indifference
then up to the glinty sea beyond —
then back. Today, for instance, prowling my glance
from open face to open face (*counts-out thirteen, each one out loud*)
before letting my animal
break free from me again.
Stars. It was stars. The prior story
lit once when there appeared to be
a master also fighting to keep
awake, fighting for total objectivity, pagan in character, fighting
towards total objectivity, what this unraveling storyline
would lead me towards: *knowing: by heart*:
under stars, by rosebush, with dog,
sometimes not among them when they fall by
                                        accident,
yet watching, still awake,
always the war at the top of the sentence, the open mouth,
always me here knowing
dew, patience, terror somewhere in my back,
also sometimes a dream but always leaping
(to stay awake) towards explanation
the way a dream will shout out (the rose-dream not
                                        the falling star)
to show by loudness it is not a wish but —
by virtue of not feeling
            created —
true — the future still so perfect there before me
      waiting

for where the first fire must be lit
to break down under it
the passage   of time

3

Until it's forcing out of time a tune a
syntax, here and here, each *here* an echo
              further along—until—
there's your signal clear and true, my queen—
(*beginning to dance, then breaking off, as lost in thought*)
but who on earth would run the news so fast?—
the god of words? rushing them onto me?
not wanting   time wasted,
tense with outstripping thought,
with the hot face of proof—idea—
so fast this loom, this long race home—
so swift the uttered reaching me
out of which I spin this listening
a form of revenge, bloodier than you'd think,
even wearing the armor of time,
even still able to cast a glance upward at
the herd looking down upon our hurry
through the apparent transparence of being—
Here it is, now. I take its meaning.

4

Dear sentence   so filled with deferral,
built on forgetting word by word how life
                      feels,
outside a garden now full of moonlight,
as if a ferocious bleeding,
asking for breathlessness, for a finishing-out
                  altogether
of thought,

using the breath down to the last broadcast—
the final strictest letting-go of seed,
                    across surface,
that the underneath might grip it,
voice filling every step of the long breath of course but it
                        still not full,
soul in it too but it still not satisfied,
link by link the thing wanting to vanquish
                    wakefulness,
even the listener, here now, you, wishing the grace
                    of finish
would weary of arrival,
taking in everything that will burn along the way—
oh look now how afraid we are as we receive
here in our throne the arrival-point, meaning,
                    about to be crowned,
that murder grow in the human heart—
how strange that it must come from the mouth
as if forced to nurse on meaning till it runs dry,
laying itself down, gauzy loomed-thing now, representation,
mind being asked to venture over it
                    in tiny footholds
one by one— ·
more than one ever wanted   to know

5

Why are the stars still there?

I see someone else becoming me

A shadow becoming me

Disfigurement of the outline-me

A furious listening

Scarcely a minute has gone by and it has me

Oh fire: softest laughter

Scorn in it   Long punishment

Ash!   Years

And how midsentence   god persists

On pauses   (a style)

And how elsewhere there is singing

Maybe a little fountain
            overhearable

Beyond the wall

You've read enough now. The path has been under
                        taken.
One hears a little of what one hears.

Looking-up, stars: when I am empty must I still
                        be?

Yes, death's game: outsideness.

The arrival leaps with its animal joy.

(and many other hours were like that)

UNDERNEATH (11)

*

By not escaping.
The future is created.

Cover me up the king whispers.
Describe the thing the king hisses.

Describe uninterrupted night. Blossoming of.
Love more ponderous than tongue.

And *how* nothing will come of nothing.
Exactly how.

Speak.

*

Altar   oracle   hearth   tribunal.
Push life up.

Give me the map there.

Know we have divided our kingdom.
Pray you undo this button

of separation

of aggregation

of the house.

Do not be reckless
                 We call it wisdom

Know we have divided our kingdom.
                 With laws drown out the cries.

Heave your heart into your mouth.
                 Bloody wedding!
                 Do not be solved.

Cover me up.
(Knife still poised at throat).

Laws of? : retaliation
           : retelling

In the style as in the action?

Bond between your cruelty and your fate:

storm of blood:

lyric memory—

So where is that wind

(do you wish to see the scar?)

(knifepoint's seeking-out of voice?)

how is that wind

to set the blood in
        motion

to choke the core of event
              out

pushing spring and the new
            shoots up

pushing the ships (at Aulis) up

into narrative then

beyond it

what can be

                   *

beyond it?

Ruin.

Realized meaning.

(*Oh mend your speech*)

Uninterrupted hiss: give map, pray you.

Exult

Describe

With one law

Cover me

from THE REFORMATION JOURNAL (2)

It was during one of these times that
I felt the midst of its suffering,

the presence of its suffering,
like a smile on a beloved face though not exactly

No one   no messenger sent   no image either

One is left to live purely by analogy

By an extreme effort of concentration

Looking just ahead to what appears to be
a pile of wretched flesh in a corner mildly brown

A bit further up the factory   the enormous debt

The sunlight very still on everything animate and in-
                                        animate
making a sound like *it is enough that you exist*

Is it not?

Is not the desire now to lose all personal will?

Come evil, my first person is hidden.

Look, I can rip it off (the pile in the
                        corner)

(once it beheld wondrous things)

(that is to say the things that are underneath)

And the narration

which relates the things

(but they must   be true)

The path of thought also now too bright

So that its edges cut

So that I'm writing this in the cold

keeping the parts from finding the whole again

page after page, unstitched, speaking for sand

Look I push the book off my desk

into the flood

"Let him be prepared to give the poison twice or
          even thrice if necessary"

As when feeling you watch my sleeping body

UNDERNEATH (SPEZZATO)

Can call me *by name*

As the keel drives onto the untouched shore

Still mindful of   earlier truths

Once son or daughter of

Now in a soldier's wind

Where one must winter

If   need   be

Technique, yes   as sure as you ever saw

Whatever god   exactly balanced

And how we must be ready for carelessness

Far from   kingdom

Slaughtered suitors on floor if you wish

Other thinking given up

Undergoing the great art   acceptance

Making music strong with weeping

Which grows fast like ivy and covers much

What cannot be endured endured or shoved up

into the heart

where the one final boundary, the river, freezes—

the northern border of it giving out

that the one-and-only stream find ultimate shape

via these our fingertips—

Light as a moth your mouth on my thigh—

The consular years

the first land-bounds, loose—

The first clear incision—

The marbles cut out—

Slaves watering the stone to cut it cleaner—

Busts hungered-out, whole bodies—

You never touched a truer stone

than this exile,

this law of finding

the inside of a shadow—

I never touched a truer stone

than this your face

stirring the wind before me

quarried from

the immensity of the good—

All round us the rustling, the miles of grain

And another face not moving we will bend for

Down out of our nationhood the fable

To the furrow of the hard *now*

Day standing by   in case needed

Both of us hands tied

half-dead from thinking

if possible sometimes muttering to the gods:

very close to the bottom of the stalk

pick   hard   love   look

PROBITY

Moves us   no end

like a wall   no end

you see a thing or two

doing the   rounds

you see

as far as it goes

the "universal"

lord how narrow

and its fist open

shopkeepers   chosen wombs

I have shown up sweet lord

have put my hand out

have looked for a long while

have run a hand along

looked for a symbol at the door

a long while

devices   prejudices

have felt for the wounds

have tired eyes

*

Easy to miss the wounds

to feel the wrong
place

not on guard

an in-between thing

ready for texture and contour

creatures appeared as if anew each day

making the case for the living god

tried putting my hand in

also   eyes

you can feel a thing or two

did the empyreal fires

were the august conjoinings

*

To wall in

to forgo the universal

how could we   how should we

does it really come to this

grey bird out my window this
                    morning as

my knowing, in the thing or two I'm made

to think, the hard journeying, my sweet mind shouldering

so willingly the impossible

as if craning forward to see round

some bend—(you should see how the appointed

take their lethal

medicine, here in Carthage

love, in

Rome) (to make themselves marble) (although some blur

even as they drink) (far from the

patria) sweet thing of mine

I hold in with my

boundaries my having watched for so long

the ruined temple wondering

how does the hallowed come down to

the swag of clay and night as a broken

arch. The bluebird cries.

*

Now there is a window here.

I have paid money for.

Also a bed.

(*Walks round and round then to and fro*).

Moving then years then walls what

is the right

order—

Wait. (*waits*).

Open palm and flatten it (*indicates*).

This is love   this enjambment (*indicates*).

Open it out to touch my back,

the slow river of my spine, press down on it,

harder now with open hand,

upon the landscape of my naked back, press down, I sleep,

the forum sleeps beneath

where as a child I caught onto the in-

advertent opening in grass where sheep were grazing and

slipped down into the tomb

of the maimed

king (of course) (ground-mist too, to make me slip)

seven stars in the sky as I go down

(*describes the firmament*)—

what does the wall contain we now must press
                                        (together)
against

if you use it to enter me more

vividly

by forcing up—

speak city—

did we align the plummets—

is the templum dead-true at intersection—

does this unequal first-world pain labor hopelessly—

does our work against the wall

tread holy circuitry—

do we establish the rudiments of an order,

a map of held back hands, gripped wrists,

the blossom of the wall,

turning our clod to will,

pressing hard,

can you feel a thing or two

did the empyreal fires

were the august conjoinings

*

You who cannot be traversed

we brave the middle kingdom of mere blossom

we numb the intelligence

we push against your law without regret

we enter my body harder because of the wall

(no labyrinth)

splayed against

free of a dying god

(what did our mothers tell)

(what does the queen of heaven know)

(what wall do they put *her* up against)

without regret

it must be done without regret

as if it were a dying empire

where the words were used up

and we now marched days into days for no
reason

without regret lord tribune

(what did the mothers tell?)

*

O labyrinth which begins with a single wall,

against which the supernatural pushes now the
open heart of a woman,

the robber with his hands flat over her palms
pushing them both back

onto the surface

where the words are used up

(where night also is but only as an ending)

(which is not what the mothers told)

(although maybe the queen of heaven)

pushing hard into that wall

that the sacred have a future

God only knows what we are holding up

two bodies all these limbs

thighs pushed to hold thighs back

against a single wall in the human universe

God only knows what it

is holding up

what it has shut in

of the outside

this wall

he's pushing up into

using her flesh

where it   ends

without regret lord tribune

to feel the end's insistence

(on war for instance)

(which he can feel through her)

we used to say it was a campaign

to the edge of   empire

it is

needed   explanation

because of the mystic nature   of the theory

and our reliance   on collective belief

I could not visualize the end

the tools that paved the way broke

the body the foundation the exact copy of the real

our surfaces were covered

our surfaces are all covered

actual hands appear but then there is writing

in the cave   we were deeply impressed

as in addicted to results

oh and dedication training   the idea of loss of life

in our work we call this emotion

how a poem enters into the world

there is nothing wrong with the instrument

as here I would raise my voice but

the human being and the world cannot be equated

aside from the question of whether or not we are alone

and other approaches to nothingness

(the term "subject")(the term "only")

also *opinion* and *annihilation*

(the body's minutest sensation of time)

(the world, it is true, has not yet been destroyed)

intensification   void

we are amazed

uselessness is the last form love takes

so liquid till the forgone conclusion

here we are, the forgone conclusion

so many messages transmitted they will never acquire meaning

do you remember   my love my archive

touch me (here)

give birth to   a single idea

touch where it does not lead to war

show me   exact spot

climb the stairs

lie on the bed

have faith

nerves wearing only moonlight lie down

lie still patrol yr cage

be a phenomenon

at the bottom below the word

intention, lick past it

rip   years

find the burning matter

love allows it (I think)

push past the freedom (smoke)

push past   intelligence (smoke)

whelm   sprawl

(favorite city)   (god's tiny voices)

hand over mouth

let light arrive

let the past strike us and go

drift   undo

if it please the dawn

lean down

say   hurt   undo

in your mouth be pleased

where does it say

where does it say

this is the mother tongue

there is in my mouth a ladder

climb down

presence of world

impassable   gap

pass

I am beside myself

you are inside me   as history

We exist   Meet me

EURYDICE ON HISTORY

1

With   what *is said*,

in this dusk   face me,

with   our muscles' work, extravagant,

as if the very pouring-out-to-sea

or the lingering motherland

that cannot recognize

its own men

or *recognize its enemies.*

Listen bitter Voice, spare part,

(also all you standing on line)

where is my master? with whom share death?

Today, shining where light is dragged away,

this small grove of young pine,

needles falling in sudden wind — and through them

a swan first on the left then on the right

of the one standing column

words carved on its base

the ripples of swan-passaging . . .

And the empty world (and the warmth of it).

And trying to see if the lips move.

2

Guilty of.

Berries eaten.

Column's last corrugation holding the light.

Children's shouts in through the

billowing.

Desire to no longer be able

to emit   sound.

Vantage point.

(The you not involved)

(Shape, yes, in-

volved) (Because it can break).

3

Have you not also let His hand stray

onto your throat?

Do you not wait for it to tighten?

What is it you await,

extended throat

song still in it?

Age of ice.   Age of iron.

Village people still standing by

for the beginning.

What will power mount now?

Do things that blossom truly wither?

Lining the streets they watch to see what justice

will become.

4

I never knew   near the end

how the world closed   and whether it *was* ever open,

punishment rustling everywhere as *it* grows thin,

sweet undergrowth with little winds in it.

How old are we now?

Chance replaces punishment.

What will be my chance?

And the first of the persons?

A woman of clay is speaking to you now,

who can kill and be killed,

like birds settling on the far field,

settling more deeply

where I close my eyes.

5

And what do I do with my laughter?

How lift and place it among the columns?

Or the swan now reversing and water reabsorbing

the new rings into the thickening old?

Are there no gods *without* mouths?

The farthest point imaginable for instance.

The heart fused with the target

as the eye draws the bow back.

The *minute-ago*

as it conjugates light.

The perfect replica . . .

The perfect replica speaks to you now.

The woman of clay;

I wanted to be broken, make no mistake.

I wanted to enter light—and everywhere its mad colors.

To be told best not to touch.

To touch.

For the farewell of it.

And the further replication.

And the atom

saturated with situation.

And the statue put there to persuade me.

NOTES

"from THE REFORMATION JOURNAL*"*: the first three lines use fragments from Gunnar Ekelof The phrases in quotation marks are from Thomas Traherne and Emily Dickinson, respectively

"UNDERNEATH (9)": Anne Carson's *Eros the Bittersweet* inspired some of the thinking and action in this poem None of the italicized lines indicate quotation

David Jones's work—especially in *Anathemata* and *In Parenthesis*—provided inspiration for this work in a very general sense "UNDERNEATH (UPLAND)" is an example of his influence in terms of tone and voice

"PRAYER *(after Holderlin)*" is built in great part of fragments from his long poems *Dichterberuf* ("The Poet's Vocation"), and *Stimme des Volks* ("Voice of the People"), in the Christopher Middleton translation

"THE SPECTATORS" is for John Ashbery

"DESERT/DUNE": the phrase "seriously wounded narrator" is from Helene Cixous

"MIDDLE DISTANCE": the first phrase in quotes is from David Jones, the second from Susan Howe

"UNDERNEATH (CALYPSO)": her name descends etymologically from the word for *veil* Hence, also, its derivate, *apocalypse* It should be apparent she is speaking to Ulysses, whom she has in thrall, as well as to us

In the poems that are dated, the dates are picked somewhat at random, in order to indicate season and duration of event

"FOR ONE MUST WANT/ TO SHUT THE OTHER'S GAZE": the title is an intentional slight misquotation from Dickinson's 640, a poem which animates the book throughout It is dedicated to Susan Howe

"UNDERNEATH (1)," "UNDERNEATH (2)," and "UNDERNEATH (3)" are influenced, musically, by Donald Revell's recent poems, to which I owe a debt of inspiration and gratitude

"UNDERNEATH (EURYDICE)": the fragment in quotation marks is a secondary quote from David Jones

"UNDERNEATH (WITH CHORUS)": owes much phrasing to David Lattimore's translation of *Oedipus Rex*

"FUSE": not so much in the language, but in its positioning of its subject, this poem owes a debt to Robert Fagles' translation of the *Oresteia*, as well as to his brilliant introduction to that book

"UNDERNEATH (11)": quotations from *King Lear* appear in stanzas four, six and seven, although the actual exploration of kingship shifts from Lear to Agamemnon and others, as it has done throughout the book

"*from* THE REFORMATION JOURNAL (2)": the phrase in quotes which constitutes the next-to-last stanza is from the death of Socrates and refers to it

"UNDERNEATH (13)": inspired by Michael Palmer's poems, this is dedicated to him

"SWARM," in *The Oxford English Dictionary*, is defined as "a body of bees which at a particular season leave the hive or main stock, gather in a compact mass or cluster, and fly off together in search of a new dwelling-place, under the guidance of a queen," as well as "persons who leave the original body and go forth to found a new colony or community "

About the Author

JORIE GRAHAM has received numerous awards for her
work, including the 1996 Pulitzer Prize for poetry for *The
Dream of the Unified Field: Selected Poems 1974 – 1994*
She was recently appointed Boylston Professor at Harvard
University and currently divides her time between
Iowa and Massachusetts